# *EXPRESSIVE FAITH*

Edited by

CHRIS WALTON

First published in Great Britain in 1999 by
TRIUMPH HOUSE
1-2 Wainman Road, Woodston,
Peterborough, PE2 7BU
Telephone (01733) 230749

All Rights Reserved

*Copyright Contributors 1999*

HB ISBN 1 86161 484 5
SB ISBN 1 86161 489 6

# *FOREWORD*

The poetry selected for this special anthology of Christian poetry holds the thoughts, feelings and emotions of many new and established writers.

Each has the special gift of being able to set a scene, share a story, or pass on a thought - providing message.

Many of the poems are true to life and cover subjects such as pain, doubt, hope and joy, along with the many other elements that make and mould our lives.

By joining hands and bringing their creativity together, a wonderful anthology has been created that offers a great wealth of inspiration and insight into the Christian way of life.

Chris Walton
Editor

## Contents

| | | |
|---|---|---|
| The Purcell Carol | John Cutter | 1 |
| Fruit Of Life | Kenneth Mood | 2 |
| Open | Robert D Shooter | 3 |
| Because Of You | Rosetta Stone | 4 |
| Shalom | John Rayne-Davis | 5 |
| Desire | J M H Barton | 6 |
| Wonder | Scarlett | 7 |
| Untitled | Katherine Rose | 8 |
| What Shall I Choose? | Mary Elizabeth Keene | 9 |
| 'Titanic' Lost Souls | Valerie Baker | 10 |
| Nature's Mind | Joan Gover | 11 |
| The Donkey's Tale | William P Hayles | 12 |
| Life's Journey | Heather Kirkpatrick | 14 |
| The Lesson Of Maundy Thursday | Anne Sanderson | 15 |
| The Scorched Earth (Via Manic Man) | Peggy Johnson | 16 |
| Blessed Is The Nation Whose God Is The Lord | Elsie Cross | 17 |
| A Pray With God | Doris Barnes | 18 |
| Childhood | Don Goodwin | 19 |
| We See The Love | Gerald Thomas Wall | 20 |
| October | Susan Goldsmith | 22 |
| Giving | William Price | 23 |
| Whose World Is It Anyway? | John Elias | 24 |
| Loving Father | Kevin Collins | 25 |
| Sacrifice And War No More | Geoff Ackroyd | 26 |
| The Golden Eagle | Noelle Hill | 27 |
| The Chestnut Tree | Pauline Butler | 28 |
| Guide Me Oh Thy Great Jehovah | Adela Llewellyn | 29 |
| Central Gift | James Leonard Clough | 30 |
| Clarkes' Gardens In The Autumn | Rodger Moir | 31 |
| My Prayer | Joan Wright | 32 |
| The Tree Of Life | Christine Barrow | 33 |
| J'Accuse | Natalie Crawshay | 34 |
| The Italian Prisoner Of War 1941 | Leonard Jeffries | 36 |
| Where The Bluebells Bloomed | Yvonne Lane | 38 |

| | | |
|---|---|---|
| Thoughts On The World | Stanley Swann | 40 |
| It Is Me | Breny Leeds | 41 |
| New Year Memories | Jean Hendrie | 42 |
| Don't Fear, Winter's Here! | Theresa Hartley | 43 |
| Accept My Little Offering | Florence Roe | 44 |
| Footsteps To Paradise | Paul 'Soul' Johnson | 45 |
| Paternoster | J H Urwin | 46 |
| The Moving On | Dorothy Mary Allchin | 47 |
| Wondrous Orb | Cheryl Blyth | 48 |
| The Artist | Peggy Seeley | 49 |
| God's Creation | Jean McGovern | 50 |
| The Welfare Officer | Susan McAuley | 51 |
| Remembered | M Williams | 52 |
| Everything Must Be | Clive G Turner | 53 |
| The Gift Of Love | Fred Arthur | 54 |
| The Queen Of Soap | T Lawrence | 55 |
| My Shepherd | Jean Beardsmore | 58 |
| Rosthewaite (After A Summer Storm) | I Calder | 59 |
| Nursing Home Lady | Marion Schoeberlein | 60 |
| Beyond The Hills | Gerry Howsin | 61 |
| Through The Window Of My Life | Margaret Scott | 62 |
| The Train Goes Speeding | Ben Hodge | 63 |
| God Knows | Denise Shaw | 64 |
| The Eyes Of Christ | Allen S Roberts | 65 |
| Would We Recognise Him | Anna King | 66 |
| And God Saw That It Was Good . . . | Jenny Proom | 67 |
| The Nun | David A Bray | 68 |
| Flight Of The Soul | Betty Furneaux | 69 |
| Did Time Stand Still? | Carol Rashid | 70 |
| Untitled II | Heather Graham | 71 |
| Faith In The Lord | Lachlan Taylor | 72 |
| One | Hilda M Evans | 73 |
| My World At 1998 | Sadie I Williams | 74 |
| Sky Scraps | Sue Garnett | 75 |
| Corcomroe Abbey, Co Clare | B J Smith | 76 |

| | | |
|---|---|---|
| The Giardino Segreto | Nicola Scott | 77 |
| The Window And The Wall | Ray Foot | 78 |
| Alone | A Pollock | 80 |
| The Lamb | Leslie Emmett | 81 |
| Faith To See | Terry Russell | 82 |
| The Wonder Of The Rainbow | Margaret Wood | 83 |
| My Dream | Alma Taylor | 84 |
| A Tribute To Life | Charles N Smith | 86 |
| Meeting | Margaret Oldman | 87 |
| I Come To The Cross | Nicky Freeman | 88 |
| Have You Ever Been Crucified | Pax | 89 |
| Christmas Thoughts | Gordon Roberts | 90 |
| The Young Ruler | Scott Moray Williamson | 91 |
| He Called Him Dad | Gerry McColl | 92 |
| Island Of Dreams | Katie Shilton | 93 |
| ΦΩΣΙΛΑΡΟΝ | Jack B Lynn | 94 |
| Galashiels | Darryl Williams | 95 |
| When The Sparrow Falls | Alison Murphy | 96 |
| Life | Sheila Cundy | 97 |
| The Living Church | Margaret McTavish | 98 |
| Here On The Ground | George A Tanner | 99 |
| Lazy | Kirsty Duncombe | 100 |
| The Garden Song | Gordon Baillie | 101 |
| Where Wild Birds Cry | Helen Perry | 102 |
| Airborne | Irvin S-Allen | 103 |
| Mysteries Of Life | Margaret Jackson | 104 |
| God Promises Peace On Earth | Ellen Cooke | 105 |
| Candlemass The Feast Of The Purification Of The Virgin | Christine Mylne | 106 |

## THE PURCELL CAROL
*(Words written to be sung to the tune of 'How Blest are Shepherds' from Purcell's King Arthur)*

On Christmas night while the still world is sleeping,
   Hush'd is Our Lord in the place of His birth:
Shepherds a lonely and cold watch are keeping,
   *Word made flesh*, God is incarnate on earth.
     Born of a Virgin obedient and blessed;
     Hail Mary! Highly favoured, be addressed.

Affrighted, shepherds are fearing no danger,
   Angelic greeting: 'Good tidings I bring:
To you is born this day, laid in a manger,
   Christ the Lord, Saviour, Redeemer and King;
     There wrap'd in swaddling clothes, find Him asleeping.'
     Silently Mary Her vigil is keeping.

Lo, in the city are steeple bells ringing,
   Glory is shining around on the hill;
High up in heaven Archangels are singing,
   'Peace on the earth be to men of goodwill;
     Glory to God in the highest,' upraising
     Their voices, and ever more Him are praising.

Come then to Bethlehem, worship before Him;
   See the great wonder the Lord hath made known;
We in heart now with the shepherds adore Him,
   Saviour of all who His kingship will own.
     Hearing these tidings men marvelled and wondered,
     Hid in Her heart Mary kept them and pondered.

*John Cutter*

## FRUIT OF LIFE

At the gardening festival I looked at leeks
And flowers.
Their beauty was marvellous.
The fruit of life.
It's a miracle how things grow.
Things are perfect by God's given hand.

I bought a raffle, tea and cake.
I sat listening and watching people talking
About the summer.
Some had success and some had failure.
Gardening is full of different designs.
There is always something new to learn
And being grateful for each season.

*Kenneth Mood*

## OPEN

Something good had died,
yet risen again,
driven to the core
there's always the door
to knock on anew
sing Hallelujah.

***Robert D Shooter***

## BECAUSE OF YOU

Because of you
I don't have to try to be
someone, something, I am not

Because of you
I can be, just me, a smile, a light,
a gentle flow

Because of you
I keep on finding me - because
I find me in you

Because of you
I see things more clearly, and with
a more vivid eye

Because of you
a rainbow is always in my heart, and fireworks
sparkle through my very being

Because of you
It is always spring, leading to
a wonderful summer

My love:
Life is
Because of you.

*Rosetta Stone*

## SHALOM

*(Inspired by a picture of a young Israeli girl
of about seven years old)*

I am the constant spirit
Of God's Holy chosen people.
Elevated but then cast down.
By pogrom, migration and holocaust.
I am the past, present and
Future, made one.

I am the spirit of Rachel
Weeping for her children.
Also I am the terrified child
In the market place after
The Hamas bomb.
I am eternity.

***John Rayne-Davis***

## DESIRE

What heart's desire, your loving hand to hold,
Would my loving heart presume so bold?
By clasp of hand, to guide love's way,
That bond so strong, for centuries lay.

What in a heart would so desire
But love, in flames of passion fire;
Your eyes have spoken, a love untold,
Honour, trust, your faith in love uphold.

From shaft of moonlight a million stars cascade
Your path to light, God has made,
For truth be such a simple thing,
Would for you, my love to bring.

Desirous but to shield, protect, avoid all hurt,
Evil thoughts or deeds, my love avert,
Would question I, my heart's desire sure,
Nought, could I love this woman more?

*J M H Barton*

## WONDER

What else to do, O Gracious Lord but kneel,
before the glories of Your wondrous art.
Not from false words of praise or senseless worship,
but with the deepest recognition in my heart.

However hard I try to understand You,
to mould a shape, a purpose to what's real,
when set before the wonder of creation,
what else to do, O Gracious Lord, but kneel.

I know not who You are, and yet I love You,
in trust I try to see what You reveal.
There is happiness and strength in my unknowing;
so with wonder in my heart, to You I kneel.

*Scarlett*

## UNTITLED

Went into the garden shed today,
haven't been there for ages.
Delicate threads of cobweb hang misted in the dew.
A snail carrying its home on its back,
behind it, a silver map of the places it's been.
Leaves, coloured with the season lay huddled in the corners,
sheltering from the cold wind that blew them there.
Bulbs lay resting,
waiting for the spring, when they will reach up to catch the golden sun.
This is their world.

*Katherine Rose*

## What Shall I Choose?

I think, if I could choose, I'd be
Attractive, strong and clever too,
A popular person, much admired,
Ahead in life's mad, jostling queue.

But would that make me useful, wise?
A cheerful person, quite content?
Oh no, God cuts me down to size,
The best for me is His intent.

Humility, God says, not pride,
Will draw friends to me, bring me peace,
In weakness I may find new strength,
From constant striving, sweet release.

A winner, God explains to me,
Loses himself and learns to give,
In serving others I will gain
The prize in knowing how to live.

I know, if I have done my best,
A failure should not bring despair
For out of it some good may come
To build me up and show God's care.

I think if I may choose again
My first ideas I'll put aside,
God's plan for me is best, I know,
He loves me and will be my guide.

*Mary Elizabeth Keene*

## 'TITANIC' LOST SOULS

Titanic on sale to the public today,
*All of her secrets - I hereto display*

On the ocean's floor she now lies at rest,
*We know, dear Lord, Captain Smith did his best*

Over two thousand passengers should have survived,
*Husbands, women, girls and boys!*

On her maiden voyage - she glided so free,
*People away from home, and misery*

Captain Smith on the platform raised,
*On his bridge for a full surveillance!*

The iceberg - unforeseen to all,
*Was Captain Smith's complete downfall!*

Lifeboats insufficient, but half,
*Panic, alarm, and bereaved mental scars*

As the bow sank deeper to the ocean's floor,
*The stern did rise - with utter panic galore!*

Titanic is no more for all to see,
*She, unsinkable, to all a mystery!*

She and her souls on the ocean's floor,
*Always in our hearts - to grieve for all . . .*

**Valerie Baker**

## NATURE'S MIND

What do we know of nature's secrets,
what view have we of her hidden treasures?
We pick the vine,
cut the grass,
prune the trees,
how much more we have to discover
When we enter into nature's mind.

We have got to be like the trees,
breezes blow and ruffle our branches,
but our trunk, our centre, remains firm and secure,
firmly fixed upon God,
knowing the oneness of all life,
letting the gales, the tempests of emotion
ruffle our leaves,
shake our branches,
but our trunk firmly grounded
in love of God and man.
When the winds and tempests cease
all will be as it was,
as it ever is,
eternally firm and true.
Let us enter into nature's mind
and leave our little human fears behind.

*Joan Gover*

## THE DONKEY'S TALE

Since leaving Nazareth we have travelled far,
Over mountains tall and pathways steep,
Guided by the westward star,
Towards Bethlehem, food and sleep.

We passed through the hills of Samaria,
At Sychar we found a place to rest,
My passenger wearied by the road so far,
Dismounted with child, this trip was a test.

A little water and hay so sweet,
Revived me, and fortified me for the road,
My passenger with child now faced the heat,
As we set off again as the cock crowed.

Past Ephraim and to the south, Jericho,
Down into the valley past Jerusalem,
Finally to Bethlehem Man and Mother go,
To find an inn to shelter them.

But the town is full and they're unable,
To find a room in the lowest of inns,
And so they join me in my humble stable,
And here the Mother's labour begins.

As I stand with sheep and cattle,
A babe is born and placed in my manger,
This Son of man, who is born to battle,
Comes into the world surrounded by danger.

The sheep and I keep a midnight vigil,
Watching over this infant of man,
He lies there sleeping, gentle and still,
To serve God's creation His ultimate plan.

I know I am only a beast of burden, an ass,
A donkey to be treated as a target for fun!
But low and behold, it then came to pass,
The Mother was Mary, the baby God's Son.

*William P Hayles*

## LIFE'S JOURNEY

Are you weary of climbing mountains
Crossing rivers
Did you notice how beautiful it was,
at the foot of the mountain
Or were you looking up at the
rugged path ahead?

When you reached the summit
Did you admire the view
Thank God for the strength to
climb it
Or were you looking down at
the river below instead?

When you arrived at the river
Did you see the sun dancing
on the water
Watch the little fish dart for
cover, under a stone?

When you reached the other side
Did you help your neighbour,
up the slippery bank
Or march on to the next mountain,
alone?

Life's journey won't last forever
Stop, admire the view
The beauty there for every eye
Is seen by only a few.

**Heather Kirkpatrick**

## THE LESSON OF MAUNDY THURSDAY

You washed disciples' feet, and we
Would never show humility
That could compare with yours, O Lord:
Such openness we can't afford.

You knew how much You would be missed,
So gave to us the Eucharist,
But how much do we really care
And honour what is present there?

You fought the inner fight alone
In stony garden to atone
For sin of men who turn their back
On You or others on the rack.

You were betrayed by Your own friends,
Yet Your forgiveness never ends:
We, too, have played the renegade,
But bear a grudge when *we're* betrayed.

While knowing the ordeal You faced,
You did not flee its bitter taste:
Such lucid courage is not ours -
We do not have Your staying powers.

Lord, raise us up now, we implore;
Transform us as You did before
With that once most unlikely crew -
Disciples who deserted You.

Today men find it hard to learn
The lessons of Your life, though yearn
To find a meaning: this they can
In You alone, O God-Made-Man.

**Anne Sanderson**

## THE SCORCHED EARTH (VIA MANIC MAN)

God, worked hard, for six whole days.
Forming the mountains, oceans and byways.
There's something missing he said to himself,
what are fruit trees, meadows and such, without any life?
So he modelled a man on himself, and called him Adam.
Then he thought, he'll be lonely,
so he took a rib from Adam, and made him a wife.
Then God rested on the seventh day, and called it the Sabbath.
How beautiful the Garden of Eden was, in those early days,
with its rippling streams and luscious fields of green.
Something today, which is becoming a dream,
but the pair defied God, and were cast out, thence the rot started,
and has carried on for thousands of years.
Their descendants fought over land, for themselves to keep,
while their kinfolk struggled, and lived in fear, who only wanted peace,
as time went on, what was built was destroyed,
warfare becoming more fierce, and destructive with advancing years.
Rain forests gone, trees felled for various goods,
sliced up to make furniture of wood,
their loss robbing people of life's necessity-oxygen,
but the biggest crime against humanity and the universe.
Was the invention of the H-bomb.
Perhaps God will become so incensed.
He'll let us know who is Master and revert the earth.
To dust and dirt.

*Peggy Johnson*

## BLESSED IS THE NATION WHOSE GOD IS THE LORD
*Psalm 33, Verse 12*

Oh great and mighty fallen
From empire far and wide
The Bible was your guide
Now the precepts you deride
God's commands no longer holds sway
for we have drifted away
Now man has his say
in the affairs of the day
Whether you eat or drink?
Or holy keep His day
It matters no more
His word shown the door
Shops open on Sunday
Even though open Monday
Church meetings small
Not with it at all
God no longer holds sway
In the affairs of the day
man's word is the law
We'll do it our way
And welcome the gay
in the services of God
as servants of His
no matter the small man
his word doesn't count
God is deposed from His reign
Did Christ die in vain?
His word doesn't count
We're shown the door
Oh how the might is fallen
Power in the world no more.

**Elsie Cross**

## A Pray With God

We may have temptations, worry and strife
Stay close to God he'll see you through life
My health remains a worry and my daughter's ill too
A whisper and a prayer the Lord will hear you
We all have worries, heartbreaks and shed tears
He will wipe our eyes and calm all our fears
Have faith in the Lord and he'll walk by your side
He will lead you to safety with arms opened wide
I walk through woods fallen leaves at my feet
Casting shadows down beyond belief
The sun surveys the earth and the sky
Keeps me safe and binds me to his side
Praise my God I am never alone he's my special friend
Each new day you give me joy in my heart
The breaking of dawn, true friendship's hand
You gave me a heart that forgives others who do wrong.
Help to show compassion with love, good and strong
God gives me strength, courage to face every day.
I thank him for my creation and my gift of life
You gave to me the gift of love and I reach to the light
Because you are the Almighty who created heaven and earth.
My Lord you came into my heart, spoke the word of God.
You prayed with me I clasped my hands for peace and joy
I thank him for loving me and all things I can behold.

*Doris Barnes*

## CHILDHOOD

Thank God for my happy childhood, the foundation stone of life.
I was so fortunate and so were my brothers and my darling wife.
We all had happy childhoods in those far off golden days.
Even though the bombs were dropping, I for one can say.
I would not swop my childhood, no, not one bit, even bombs and all.
We never had no sweets or money, but we were so happy I do recall.
We could go to the woods all day, we were not afraid of men.
Because every grown-up looked out for us, and then
We all had discipline, we knew what was right and wrong.
And we were part of a real family, and we knew that we belonged.

***Don Goodwin***

## WE SEE THE LOVE

We see the love in the man
Who came to take our place,
Our sins led to His torment,
Our sins led to death's embrace.
Mocked, humiliated, condemned,
Whipped even to His bones,
Yet His lips remained silent,
Enduring alone.

We see the love in His brow
Pierced by twisted thorns,
Our sins led to His torment,
Our sins led to His crown.
His head bore the marks
Which indeed we should own,
Because of His wonderful love for us
He wore the crown alone.

We see the love in His hands
Pierced by sharpened nails,
Our sins led to His torment,
Our sins led to His pain.
His palms bear the marks,
Etched for all to see,
Love is in His pierced hands,
What love, O joy, how free!

We see the love in His body
Battered and broken for us,
Our sins led to his torment,
Our sins led to His cross.
Even through the agony
He had no intention to complain,
He bore our sins silently,
For our sins this Lamb was slain.

We see the love in His blood
Shed to cover our sins,
Our sins led to His torment,
Our sins led to His pain.
But by His blood we are forgiven,
By His blood we are made free,
Jesus died - yet has risen,
He gives life - liberty.

***Gerald Thomas Wall***

## OCTOBER

Gazing through the window, upon this October day
Brings such amazement, how nature works and plays
Silver streams of cobwebs, clinging from the stars
Rainbows dancing as sun shines, through a crystal vase

Many flying insects, dashing here and there
So many different birds, taking to the air
The prettiest leaves gently, floating to the ground
Blue tits pecking at nut bags, they have readily found

There are breezes softly blowing, yet the sun is gently warm
So many wasps all alone, no longer in a swarm
Dewdrops hang as the willow sways
A butterfly seems to have lost its way

Bronzed and ruddy autumn leaves
Adorned the once greenest trees
Little robin never stopping
From trees and bushes he keeps popping

Berries richer than precious rubies, webs dusky with dew
Through your window God, do you see all that's wonder, old and new?
Maybe just death and destruction, meets your saddened eyes
Take time to peek Lord, through the windows of your skies

At one little garden God, before autumn tires
And frost forms upon the tallest of your spires
Such wonders there will help, to unburden your heart
For in your weary task again, you must make a start.

**Susan Goldsmith**

# GIVING

The world has many happy folk who smile each day they live.
Because they've found that happiness depends on what you give,
For a giving man is different from his neighbour in the pod
When his thoughts are of his brothers . . .
Then he's closest to his God.

And the spark of love he kindles in a breast
Where hope has died,
Sheds a warmth like no other . . .
For it feels so good inside.

And everything he gives a bit he adds a
Little part
To that something deep within him . . .
That the poets call a heart.

***William Price***

## WHOSE WORLD IS IT ANYWAY?

Have you seen a 'Star of David' with its mesh of royal blue
And shimmering creamy halo - o'er leaves of soft green hue
Have you watched the small buds open with delicate grace each day
To reveal the translucent glory of the golden fruits display
A million, trillion species of plants meet mankind's needs
But who - 'tis often wondered wisely planted the first seeds?

Have you heard the skylarks' diva trill - in the cold, grey dawn
                                    when the world stands still
Seen the swallows dive - a robin's breast - the soft-shelled eggs
                                    in a blue tit's nest
The peacock's splay - a rainbow bright - heard the nightgale's song
                                    on a moonlit night
A myriad birds fill the world with song - but from whence
                                    came the first small egg along?
And all the fishes of the sea - how is it that they came to *be*?
Animals, reptiles, creatures small - how is it that they're here at all?
Are they products all of 'evolution'? Are brainier *planets* the solution?
Raining down upon the earth - acorns, seeds, *all* things of birth?
The problem, the logician faces - then who created the planets' races?

It seems quite clear that there must be - a power greater than you and me
Who created a world of wonder and grace - with undying love
                                    for the human race
With all the evidence it's sad and odd - that some can't accept
                                    the existence of God.

*John Elias*

## LOVING FATHER

Loving Father in heaven, watch over our child tonight.
Soothe his pain, till the early morning light.
Dry his painful tears, with your loving hand.
If he goes to heaven above, we'll try to understand.

Send down your love, the gentlest of all.
Please help our child, so helpless, so small.
He means the world, to his mother and me.
His world is dark, for he is blind you see.

His little body is filled with so much pain.
Our hearts are hurting over and over again.
We pray to you loving Father, our little boy means so much.
So small are the fingers, that give a gentle touch.

I know I am not worthy, though I pray to you now.
He is our world, please help him stay some how.
His gentle breathing, the pain he is going through.
Hear our words loving Father, as we pray to you.

Dawn comes through his window, night-time has ceased.
Our little boy is in heaven, now he sleeps in peace.
In our hearts he will remain, though he's in heaven above.
Jesus needed another angel, in His kingdom of pure love.

*Kevin Collins*

## SACRIFICE AND WAR NO MORE

Mostly in their youth and splendour
they have fallen in our name.
For a cause they often doubted,
zeal for peace and not for fame.

In the noise and rage of battle
or the cruel sea and tide.
In the air with cruel cargo
wore their uniform with pride.

Taken from their home or family
to battle in a time of war.
Far away in foreign landscape
rest they there for ever more.

Forgive them Lord if by their actions
a brother of the foe has died.
Both will now be there in glory
together marching side by side.

Lord comfort those, because of conflict
have families and homes destroyed.
Refugees along the highway,
nurses caring, the unemployed.

Lord take from the nations the need of battle
bury the spear, the sword and guns.
Settle their differences round Your great table,
Sacrifice ceased of daughters and sons.

*Geoff Ackroyd*

# The Golden Eagle

Emblem of nations, wayward wanderer of the air,
Whose hooded eyes, undazzled scan the distant height,
To where the wary vixen, watches in her lair;
Piercing beyond the confines of reflected light.

Swiftly he circles o'er his chosen one, her dower
Of broken feathers falling, as the pair cavort,
Spiralling around them in ever gath'ring shower;
Trophies of their courtship, favours dearly bought.

Mounting on russet wings where strands of gold are spun,
'Jove's Thunderbolt' that strikes the hammer-blow of fate,
Grey as a threat'ning cloud, looms large against the sun.
His victim, frozen in his tracks, can only wait.

Caught by the cruel beak, torn by talons sharp as steel,
He falls, limp and helpless, with a last shudd'ring sigh.
Straightway to his eyrie, his prowess to reveal,
The eagle bears his prey, as length'ning shadows die.

His mate in patient vigil, wond'ring at his stay,
Guards an untidy round branched nest, of twigs and pine,
Cradled in moss, her spotted, goose-like eggs she'll lay.
Hatched by her body, plucked and bare. A lone ensign

In a tall tree, rising above the dark abyss;
Lost in the snow-capped, crested peaks, she dwells among.
When hazy summer days dissolve, with autumn's kiss,
The fledgling eaglets, flound'ring, from the nest are flung.

Their mother's back serves as a launching pad in space,
A vital pivot in a noble master-plan.
Exiled from home, they set off with an easy grace,
Alone, resolved the compass of the earth to span.

*Noelle Hill*

## THE CHESTNUT TREE

Tall, her noble boughs outspread
Embracing sun and wind and rain
She lifts her lovely leafy head.
Gives thanks to God for life again.

Gives thanks for life held in her hands
Green buds that open day by day
Until they burst their prickly bands
Then swift and silent fall away

To Mother Earth from whence they came
Who welcomes each and every one
As she will too, our mortal selves
When our brief span on earth is done.

But this we know is not the end
No death or dreary decaying here
Come spring and clothed in green again
Sends out her message loud and clear.

Life will go on, the day will come
When like the lovely chestnut tree
We too will rise and praising God.
Will enter our eternity.

*Pauline Butler*

## GUIDE ME OH THY GREAT JEHOVAH

Dear God put kindness in my heart today
So no act of mine may lead someone astray
Let me talk with a healing tongue
In myself help put aside the wrong

Keep me awake to other people's needs
Help me to keep the path where Jesus leads
Point me to right so I will surely see
Not as I am but as I want to be

Help me never to speak of things to hurt
Always to your voice to be alert
To work with cheerfulness and not give in
To work your way and your pleasure win

Not to let anger get control of me
Keeping calm where anger's all I see
Be unafraid when trouble heads my way
Knowing you are with me all the way

Jehovah I put all my trust in you
You are always there no other friend so true
Help me to be worthy of your love and care
I can climb mountains if you are there.

**Adela Llewellyn**

## CENTRAL GIFT

Give your revealing word to minds discerning,
Christ's kingdom of justice, liberty and peace.
Chart for warring nations with homesteads burning,
Centre of mercy, inventive hope increase.
When greed and carnage leave a country shaken,
Guardian care, to goodwill, people awaken.

Join us all Gracious Spirit with one accord,
Like the rainbow colours of earth's creation.
You come in power promised by our Victor Lord,
Forgiven, renewed, inward transformation;
One fellowship of partners without ending,
Throughout the world all races truly blending.

Strengthen our toil Creator of light and power,
Aiding our work with diligence every day.
Teach us not to neglect small tasks or cower,
Striving for excellence, your wonders display.
True honour for earth's work-force shall be restored,
Blest the land whose great endeavour brings concord.

Praise loving Lord for each new day of free grace,
Guiding us with inner truth to all things fair.
When mists impede, Love keeps us in sure embrace,
Where sundered friends still are one in heart and prayer.
For faith's sight, doubts, denials never avail,
Who trusts Easter morning thrill, always prevail.

Thanks Comforter divine, joy of happy hearts,
No hazard stops your love flowing in splendour.
Joy comes to us in friends, children, purest arts.
The Light of the world shines as our Defender.
Beyond pain and death is emancipation,
Held by Love we share Heaven's jubilation.

*James Leonard Clough*

## Clarkes' Gardens In The Autumn

Clarkes' Gardens is at its best this time of year
Brilliant white fills my windows
Everything glistens in October
Shades of darkest green and gold unfold
And fill up the pathway for months on end
A sense of melancholy sweeps my brain through
As winter with its clammy hands
Threatens to make the days shorter
Squeezing out the sunlight
But I'll make snowmen with snow
And I'll dance in its rain
I'm determined that this winter
Won't bring me down again
But I still love the autumn though
And enjoy it while it lasts
How can I not love October
As I walk Clarkes' Gardens path

**Rodger Moir**

## MY PRAYER

With eyes closed and bowed head
This is my prayer I've often said
I thank you Lord for each new day
Thank you for the warmth of the sun's golden rays.

Thank you for each hour of precious light
For the watch you keep over me through the night
For the beauty of the skies
That fills my heart and mind with delight.

Thank you Lord for letting me eat
When there's many have no meat
They have no place to rest their head
When I am tucked up warmly in my bed.

Thank you for listening when I pray
Often only in my hour of need
I know I am guilty of that greed
Yet expect an answer to my pleas.

You give me so many things
Much richness to my life it brings
I know I don't deserve it all
For what I give in return is so very small.

*Joan Wright*

# THE TREE OF LIFE

There is a tree, a tree which shadows.
All within its range,
A giant in surroundings humble,
For centuries standing without change.

There is a tree, a miracle,
A prodigy of nature,
Standing alone 'midst barren land,
Majestic in its stature.

There is a tree with branches wide
They span five hundred feet,
Erect within the desert sands
Against the searing heat.

From whence the seed from which it grew,
From whence its nourishment,
Beneath the desert driven deep
Its probing roots were sent.

The seeds were carried on the wind,
And by some miracle,
The ground absorbed and nurtured one
When down to earth it fell.

By chance, a spring deep under sand,
Gave life to sapling weak,
Strengthening and transforming it,
Into a desert freak.

There is a tree, spectacular,
Where visitors are rife,
Just to view this miracle,
Known as 'The Tree of Life'.

**Christine Barrow**

## J'ACCUSE

I dreamed I was called in the dead of the night
to the local police, and, oh, what a fright
when I got there to witness a line-up of men
who I knew very well (you can say *that* again!)

They'd all done me wrong at some point in my life
The pain they had caused me *I'd* call more than strife
All used and abused me, then tossed me aside
on the road to recovery, stripped of my pride

The officer told me 'You must pick him out,
the person to blame, who most made you doubt
there existed a man who *could* treat you right -
we'll tear him apart with all of our might!'

I stared at the officer, and he back at me
'You *must* do this deed or you never will see
retribution for all of the wrongs they have done,
but you can't pick them all - it can only be one'

'Choose very carefully and you will soon find
the rest of your love-life will turn out just fine
All future men will think twice, even thrice
before using *your* passion like cats teasing mice'

'The message will reach all mankind far and wide
You'll wear your heart proudly, not cower and hide
in case each has potential to do you more harm
Don't be afraid,' he said, 'Here, take my arm'

So we faced them together, one fiend and all
as I strutted past each of them, head lifted tall
And when we had doubled right back to the start
he yelled 'Do it *now*, and reclaim your heart!'

So I lifted my hand and formed a strong finger
But something within me made my hand linger
Then everyone gasped for they clearly could see
my hand had turned 'round - I was pointing at me!

*- The Beginning -*

**Natalie Crawshay**

## THE ITALIAN PRISONER OF WAR 1941

For all that's gone I still recall his face.
My sole excuse, I was not twenty-one
and spirited by war. Had he refused
I would have put my bayonet through his neck,
yet all I wanted was his neckerchief:
such proud possession when you count his stock
as this and makeshift shorts and ragged shoes.

He, ravaged by the war and desert sands,
a prisoner, ridiculed, beneath contempt,
with swarthy Latin features, Latin skin,
thirsting for drink, weak from the lack of food,
could still afford a fraction of dissent
whilst losing his protection from the sun.

What was that look he gave, subservience?
A hint of fear? A moment of despair?
No, none of these, for even now I feel
that look was something he could not repel,
for as his comrades stood, depleted, done,
the faintest breath of courage skimmed his face:
a slight bravado, sort of facial shrug:
something that didn't warrant reprimand
yet haunted all my life with its content,
for here I saw whatever strength the man
will matter not when comes the final blow,
for, finished, he will scrape some dignity
from a subconscious source: the clown will clown,
the weeper weep, the hero draw his sword,
the boaster boast, and this one does contend
to flaunt his base bravado to the grave:
to act his part, though dangerous is the scene,
and seek applause down to the bottom step.

This man, this fleeting moment of my life,
would scarce survive the ravages of war
yet he is with me still, has cautioned me
and taught me to obey life's principles:
been through a second's glance
both mentor and conductor of my life.
That I had no compunction over his.

***Leonard Jeffries***

## WHERE THE BLUEBELLS BLOOMED

Sing a song of hypermarkets, shopping trolleys row on row.
Kippers, eels and trays of frogs' legs, pickles, spices, fresh baked
dough.
Tins of this and pots of that, neatly stacked together,
Socks and vests and pants and tights, coats for colder weather.
All requisites for your pet - from worming pills to hay,
Dustbins, dustpans, tools for work and also games for play.
Fish cake, cream cake, mop and pail, also carpet sweeper,
(And if you'd like to serve yourself, you'll buy your petrol cheaper).
TV sets and freezer fridges, soap and baby foods;
Save your bus fares, see the cheap wares - all these goodies:
Who wants woods?

Chorus:
'Jingle tills, jingle tills, jingle every day, we will do our weekly shopping
in the woods today'.

Lament:
Gone the squirrel from the beech tree, gone the dormouse from his
home;
Gone the badger and the rabbit, gone the path where fox would roam.
Gone 'Dawn Chorus', hymn of praise that welcomed each new day,
Gone nightingale - we loved to hear you sing the night away.
Gone grey pigeon from the treetop, raucous jay and collared dove,
Magpie, chaffinch, darting wren, those speckled eggs we used to love.
Gone the chestnut, beechnut, hazel; gone wild strawberry, blackberry,
sloe.
Gone the ash, the elm, the yew trees. Years it took for you to grow.
Gone the wandering woodland pathways, gone the banks of chalk land
flowers,
Gone the peace, the smell of leaf mould, where we spent such God
filled hours.

From the needles of the larches, wood ants built their nests so high,
But like the birds, the beasts, the beetles, man decreed that they must
die,
Gone the birthright of our children - pure air, freedom, room to play.
Here instead, pollution, tensions, noise and traffic jams all day.
Let's 'sing a dirge' for long lost bluebells, fill your trolleys, count
the cost.
All the goodies in the world will not make up for what we've lost.

**Yvonne Lane**

## THOUGHTS ON THE WORLD

No matter what the time of day
Make time as to God we pray
Thank him for this world of beauty
Appreciation is your only duty

Look at nature's every aspect
Tallest tree to smallest insect
Each one playing a crucial part
Just as they have right from the start

We take for granted so many things
Fish that swims and bird that sings
God the provider to all our needs
Fruit and flowers or just plain seeds

The water cycle turns clouds to rain
Man then pollutes again and again
Waterfalls nearing perpetual motion
Down the rivers to the ocean

This tried and tested recipe
As God replenishes the sea
The creatures of the sea are waiting
Everyone anticipating

Is this part of a cosmic pattern?
Ruled by Jupiter or Saturn
Where God will have his final say
As the tide he turns today.

*Stanley Swann*

## IT IS ME

I stumble through mists on horizons afar,
Ever straining to see through the veil of my sin,
Helpless and longing to be where You are,
Knowing what I must lose Your glory to win
And the soul that is lost where the sky meets the sea
Dearest Lord, it is me, it is me.

I want to walk in the footsteps of Jesus your Son,
I want to reach out my hand and to touch this deep pain,
I want to breathe in the breath of the one that was shun,
I want to wash in His blood 'til my soul's free from stain
And the soul that was cleansed by His blood on that tree
Dearest Lord, it is me, it is me.

Can I step to Your beat, can I march to Your drum
That is rhythmically pounding a pulse in my brain?
Can I blot out the din of this world's deadly hum,
Can I sing Your sweet song my soul to sustain
And the heart in Your hand that is beating so free
Dearest Lord, it is me, it is me.

This world is Your tapestry woven so fine
With the colours and hues that are rich and so bright.
All that is Yours, You have given as mine
And Your stars shine like jewels on the canvas of night.
And the one with the jewels that are shining for Thee
Dearest Lord, it is me, it is me.

I want to tread the sure road that will lead to Your door,
As I sing of Your wonders, Your power and Your might,
I want to tell someone else of the love that's so pure
That can save this dark world by Your spirit of light
And that soul reaching heaven Your glory to see
Dearest Lord, is it me? Is it me?
O Lord, dearest Lord, make it me.

*Breny Leeds*

## NEW YEAR MEMORIES

New Year, for me, nowadays,
Is not the same thrill any more,
50 years ago, just after midnight,
I'd have, lots of 'first-foots' at my door.

I used to wish, that my 'first-foot',
Would always be, dark and tall,
Because I was told, that a fair haired one
Brought no luck at all.

Everyone brought shortbread, or a bottle,
When they used to call,
Or sometimes a 'kipper', dressed in tissue paper,
To hang up, on your wall.

We all used to, enjoy ourselves,
Dancing and singing, all night long,
Laughing and joking, with our friends,
And taking turns, to sing a song.

But now, I'm widowed, and getting old,
And don't have parties any more,
So I know, there won't be, any 'first-foots',
Knocking at my door.

So now, I say 'Happy New Year', to my little dog,
Have a cup of tea, and go to bed,
'Cos there's no celebrations, nowadays,
So I live, on memories instead.

*Jean Hendrie*

## DON'T FEAR, WINTER'S HERE!

Wet, windy and blustery
In fact, it's blowing a gale
Cold, damp, miserable
No good for a sail
Puddles, blowing branches
Condensation, no elation
Winter's here, now this year
Curl up in front of an open fire
Cosy, warm and full of desire!

*Theresa Hartley*

## ACCEPT MY LITTLE OFFERING

Accept my little offering,
Oh Lord who rules on high,
The God who made the heavens,
Who raised the mountains high,
You, who set the stars in space
And formed the baby small,
Came Yourself a babe to be
Within a cattle stall.

Oh joy of God incarnate
Arisen from the dead,
The presence of your spirit
By whom I am daily led.
The voice of all creation
Proclaims you Christ the Lord!
What glory's in the heavens,
What comfort in your word.

My precious loving Jesus,
In me for evermore,
Blest sharing with your people,
And heaven's still in store!
What fountains these of gladness,
To cheer my gloomiest days,
Oh open then my lips, Lord,
To offer heartfelt praise.

***Florence Roe***

## FOOTSTEPS TO PARADISE
*(A tribute to Walter Whitehead)*

The flowers and the trees,
Will give you sweet inspiration.
The birds and the bees sing in harmony.
Beauty all around as you walk on solid ground.
Keep on walking and your heart will not be broken.

Don't be afraid of the dark,
Think of all the happy children playing in the park.
Life is like a journey,
Not knowing which way you want to go.
Standing at the cross-roads,
No sign to make up your mind.
Nobody knows where the wind blows,
Is it fate or is it your destiny?
Keep your chin up and you will find
Your own identity.

The gladness in your eyes,
Will wash away the sadness you feel inside.
The touch of your fingertips in your hair,
It will show you the way to 'heaven on earth'.

Think of all the beauty,
Surrounded by the world unite.
Like painted coloured butterflies,
That hover in the night.
Lovey, dovey in the sky,
Is watching over you, with love and pride.

Sweet dreams and prayers,
It is only the answer to, at the top of the stairs.
Don't think of darkness, think of light.
God is taking care of you,
On this lonely, lonely night.

**Paul 'Soul' Johnson**

## PATERNOSTER

Father above,
Send us your love;
May all obey
Your will alway.

Give us, we pray,
Our needs this day;
Give us reprieve,
As we forgive.

Keep us from sin,
Pure hearts within;
Now and always,
We give you praise.

Amen.

*J H Urwin*

## THE MOVING ON

The mood of the season is changing now.
Why should summer keep on smiling her golden smile,
if she no longer wishes to do so?
Why should it shine with happiness of sun,
when the season is change of mood?

Her brows of clouds above her glistening eyes,
are gathering now.
Why shouldn't her faceless sky cry tears
if she wants to?

Much rain is due,
and Autumn wants to wade her sombre coloured feet
into it through pools of rain.
Autumn's leaves; yellow, brown from now leafless trees
will fill the bill, now;
The water torrents will soak
and absorb it all at last.

The start of autumn is weird at the beginning,
dark of night;
The phantoms collect before the 'maybe' promise of white snow
comes to sink within winter:
The occult direst black
evil spins around to haunt us, all;
before the pure cleansing month of Christmas.
Christ's Mass comes sacredly to supremely help
with Redeeming *Christ!*

**Dorothy Mary Allchin**

## WONDROUS ORB

We are a giant orb,
nestled in the sky.
Peering at our neighbours,
as we travel always by.

Transfixed am I,
clustered to amongst the stars.
Watching the night sky,
for Jupiter or Mars.

The essence of God sinks into our oceans,
or lays thick upon the ground.
He's always near us,
yet no sight, nor sound.

God's companion, friend and relation to the earth,
father to us all since birth.
Creating so many different faces,
pulling seas in foreign places.

Forever God will remain,
always silent,
yet always the same.

*Cheryl Blyth (18)*

## THE ARTIST

I was going to a meeting
And as I closed the door
The sky above the rooftops was alight.
The day had been quite murky
But the clouds had rolled away
And the sunset was a truly wondrous sight.
I wished I'd had a canvas
And a palette full of paints
The colours were a glory to behold
Turquoise, lemon, palest pink
And floating over all
Small shining clouds of silver and of gold.
I've dabbled as an artist
And my skies aren't bad at all
But I doubt that I could capture what I saw
God had taken up *His* palette
And produced this glorious sight
Which made me stop and filled me full of awe.
And all his work around us
In the sky or on this land,
On the mountain, in the river or in wood
All send the same old message
About this beauteous land -
God made it, and he saw that it was good.

**Peggy Seeley**

## GOD'S CREATION

God made everything through the skies and land
Through His wondrous ways and powerful hand
When springtime arrives, and brightness appears
The miracles of the sun clears the mist away, as it disappears

When the skies are clear, and the blackbirds are seen
Through the woodlands, and the gardens and dewy green
As they sing out their notes full of cheer
Harsh notes are heard, so very clear

Repeated lengthy periods, of 'pink pink', of a high pitch cry
Waking up the other birds, but soon to fly through the sky
While, the thrush sits listening on her leafy bough
Swinging to and fro, while the soft winds blow

She greets the sun, with her sweet songs of praise
A chattering flute call, whistling between each phrase
Peeping this way, and that way, then back to her nest
Protecting her off-spring, under her creamy breast

While, the jay sings out his warbling song, on a warm clear day
Where the squirrels come out of the willows to play
Chasing each other, then boldly they climb
Up and down trees, that blossom with lilac and lime

Until they have a picnic, with nuts galore
With outstretched paws, they then ask for more
While the willows lift their leaves up and down so gently
Showing God's works, and signs of beauty

Oh, such blessedness, as the best things in life are free
To the voices of the birds, and the whispers of the trees
When we listen to the calls of birds, that give so much pleasure
Especially when we know that God is the great creator.

*Jean McGovern*

## THE WELFARE OFFICER

She sits in judgement,
Listening, but not hearing, a word they say.
She has her own notions about the poor
'Give them nothing, let them work like everybody else'

She hears their story,
She has heard it all before.
She's tired of these lowly people
Always looking for handouts and yet for more.

In her own mind, she'll give them nothing,
Make them suffer, make them crawl,
Make them work hard, and they won't come back for more.
Yes, she's a tight fisted woman, stern to the core.

She never got past Leaving Cert. Herself . . .
But she worked hard, got to where she is,
She's righteous, knows it all . . . knows their kind.

But she is blind to her own ignorance
Knows nothing about the poor.
She doesn't know and doesn't want to know anyway.
For she is tired of these dreary people,
She wishes they would all just go away.

If they think she is unfair,
Not treating them as she ought,
They daren't raise their voices and needn't think to ever shout.
For she will call in her hench men
The ones the mob call the shade (police).
From where the poor stand, ignorance stems from the top down.

*Susan McAuley*

## REMEMBERED

I wish my love was here by my side,
As the golden autumn fades, winter's on the way,
To tell of vegetables which won first prize,
And show off the last red rose of summer's bloom,
And hear humorous jokes banishing winter's gloom.
Now daffodil and tulip bulbs planted, rest in deep rich soil.
I alone appreciate the hard hours of toil.
I wish my love was here by my side,
To watch our daughter walk down the aisle.
The bridal gown, traditional white,
Our daughter smiled at me, a radiant s mile,
Then bridesmaids posed to the photographer's delight.
A gusty breeze lifted the fragile veil which soared,
Slim fingers caressed the delicate freesia which both adored.
I wish my love was by my side,
To give a re-assuring smile and hold my hand,
Through unshed tears I know you're near and understand.
I love my daughter but loved you more,
It was a perfect wedding except for that flaw,
But life goes on and time heals pain,
I'll always remember my love, until we meet again.

*M Williams*

## EVERYTHING MUST BE

Everything must be,
To belong to the sea,
The sea of knowledge,
To be free,
Free of karma,
On a sunny day,
Jewels of knowledge,
We so happily play,
Thoughts focus up above,
God loves us so much,
The light of the day,
We need to touch,
One day the sun will come,
A day of joy,
A day to be home,
Everything must be.

***Clive G Turner***

## THE GIFT OF LOVE

Pure is the light of morning, as the sun dries away the mist of the dawning. One day someone had prayed, that love would come along, just like the beauty of a lovely song, with the words, *'No other one could ever have your charm, that delights, and warms the heart!'*
Devotion filled their true love, so warm and cherished, from the very start, but one day they had to part, just like an ache, that breaks the heart.
Some people may forget you, as the years of time go by, but others will remember you, with a tear, and a smile.
Looking at the lovely flowers, dressed up in the beauty of their colours, a token of a loving gift, with the words *'How much you are missed'*.
The flowers are left by your side, and a kiss is thrown within one's mind, to hide the sadness within the eyes, for the tear drops that have been cried.
Love grows stronger, whilst one is far away, in the land of a beautiful place, that's where you gently wait, for the day, when love returns, one coming day.
In dreams of nights that are calling, loneliness awaits to fill the day, of morning.
Blessed are the prayers, that are said within the church, for our Lord to hear their words, and the silent whispered thoughts.
Love, and peace, were the written words, of our Lord's life story, so divine is the heart of faith, that awaits, for the heavenly glory.
Lonely is the path, that is walked once more, with the cherished memories, that are deep, within their thoughts.
Just for a while were those words spoken, once from time, to meet again, in the same old way.
*'That outstanding day!* . . . *'One perfect day!'*

**Fred Arthur**

## THE QUEEN OF SOAP

Soap but you never had a wash or a bath
Soap without water
Evolution of language?
Or a slip of the tongue?

Can you smell life?
Unshaven, unwashed
Escape mundane reality for a night
The scattered word, wide audience
Eagerly, anxiously watch

Nosey Parker
With a large enormous nose
Look like a parrot
Hot gossip over the garden wall

Reliving, reciting
Over and over relating the events
A fantastic fantasy
A reflection of every day reality
Just an every day trivial event

It is rumoured
But never denied
HM the Queen
And the corgis
Switch on the box
To escape from palace every day life

Rover's Return
Need a dog actor
With four legs
To sleep next to the bar
As the customers chat
In the most famous pub in the land

I love the cat
A purr-fect natural act
Is he an actor?
Or just merely a cat?

Pints of ale supped
As the actors lean on the bar
The lady actresses sip mother's ruin
Gin and tonic, served by the barmaid
In the lounge

Roll! Action! Camera!

This is not yesterday's script
Written by Shakespeare from the past
Was he alive? Even he could
Not write a more popular, classic act

The famous shop on the corner
Mike Baldwin's sweatshop
Hum with a buzz
Shopkeepers, mechanics
Are just some of the stars

A bored housewife
Earning pin money
By being a part-time
Porn star

The scriptwriter
Playing the role of God
For the scriptwriter
Decides the faith, the destiny of the stars

Love, hate, lust, incest
Red Rum can you spell?
Right to left?
An adulterous tale with a *gay* twist
Reflecting life's trivial events

Deirdre went to jail
A tale of love and deceit
I hoped secretly
The judge, the jury shall keep her
Behind bars
For at least a year and a day

Block, black capitals
In South Africa
Headlines the picture
Of the actress
Behind bars

The editor
Such a highly paid gent
Either a smart ass,
Or a penny short of a bob?

Could he not tell?
This is fantasy bordering
On the edge of reality
Make believe
Merely a fabulous act!

Escape reality
Switch on the box
Switch off the brain
Enter the twilight zone
Of reality, that stops you going insane
On the streets of Manchester's fame

**T Lawrence**

## MY SHEPHERD

The Lord is my Shepherd
He's with me everywhere
If I'm glad and happy
Or sad and in despair

He's never far away from me
If I'm fearful and alone
He's always showing me His love
He's my King upon the throne

He always shows the way to me
The path that I should choose
Directing me along life's way
In case my way I lose

For He wants me to become
A true follower of Him
So I can help other lives
Be rid of all their sin

He paid the biggest price
To set all people free
He pleads with people *everywhere*
*I'm the good Shepherd*
*Turn to Me*

**Jean Beardsmore**

## ROSTHEWAITE (AFTER A SUMMER STORM)

The sun slid out from behind a cloud
and cast its rays upon the ground,
colours of amber, mauve and green
by mortal eye should not be seen
hues that lay upon the land
painted by an angel's hand.
What bliss if heaven would be like this.

*I Calder*

## NURSING HOME LADY

Flowers of pain
shine in her eyes,
the old lady
in the nursing home
sings a senile song.
She keeps singing
until the nurses
quieten her with medicine,
and then she sleeps
like a dead flower
under her quilt,
dreaming of someone
loving her.

*Marion Schoeberlein*

## BEYOND THE HILLS

Beyond the hills and far, I strode
With no such place, abode
Top to tail of threadbare clothes
Careless and on, I rove

With aid of staff, I crossed a road
And on and on I strode
My swag, an awesome, tiresome load
I sighed, a moment, I froze

From where I stood, leaped a large, green toad
I staggered, for why, God knows
The toad - it croaked and quietly posed
Walked on, heard squawking of crows

Soon shall daylight surely close
Likes of petals of a fallen rose
Skies shall darken and bats in drones
Are sure to arrive, eat flesh from the bone

Beyond the hills and far, I strode
With no such place, abode
'Neath the sun, by day I rove
By night - I meet my foe.

*Gerry Howsin*

## THROUGH THE WINDOW OF MY LIFE

I've been here in my bedroom, confined mostly to my bed
And all my fears, my hopes and joys keep running through my head
The soft white sheets, not harsh and cold, starched without any feeling
A multi-coloured eiderdown in places its feathers revealing
The chairs, the pictures, the curtains have all shared my secret feelings
The well worn bible and hymn book too, from which my praises
Reached the ceiling
And in my times of trouble with pain so hard to bear
A loving family cares for me, yes, they are always there
My eyes search for a wider world beyond the window frame
And I can see such wondrous things beyond the latticed pane
Sometimes the sky is dark and dull with mist and falling rain
And in the winter icicles form, then the scene changes again
But oh the spring and summer are my favourite time of year
With blue skies in the distance and then blossoms all appear
The honeysuckle snuggles close, climbing toward the roof
Hollyhocks, lupins and sunflowers, stand proud and so aloof
Some day, as I gaze outside this window frame
I'll heave a sigh, my soul will rise, my body will remain
I'll fly outside the bedroom and go on through the door
Pass the window, see myself, but not sad like before
I can roam among the tall green trees and smell the wayside flowers
See rabbits, butterflies and bees and make up for wasted hours
Then like a bird I'll soar on high, but don't be sad for me
For you have given me precious love and now my spirit's free
I'll soar on heavenward to meet my friends and this is where my
Journey ends
I'll reach that meadow with lamb and dove and there I'll dwell
In the *land of love.*

**Margaret Scott**

## THE TRAIN GOES SPEEDING

The train goes speeding down the line
Oh! I wish it arrived on time
The steam if puffs into the air
It goes as fast as it dares
The train slipped, off came a wheel
And from the lines the train did spill
The passengers fell out the doors
They fell right down onto the floor
The train rolled down the hill and slowly stopped
The passengers climbed on-board
They did hop to one side of the train
To balance it, they set off again
They made the station with great surprise
We're all glad they'd not lost their lives.

*Ben Hodge (7)*

## GOD KNOWS

Dear God know please that the people are getting restless,
Their burdens are making them listless.
They have no balance, like a ship at sea.
From the wind that is blowing they can't find the lee.
They've not been trained to plot a course.
To flee from the wind that blows with such force.
Unstable and unsteady in this turbulent life
Deeply drowning unable to flee from strife.
Sucked into a vortex, spinning like leaves in a thrashing storm.
Relentlessly driven by an unseen form.
Dear God please be aware
And show to these people your loving care.
For it is written that you know their plight
And that they are never far from your perceptive sight.
So in this vortex, this maelstrom of iniquity and sin,
Teach them what they need to know in order to win.
To face the challenges so as to forge ahead.
To give them peace instead of dread.
To settle their fears and centre their hearts
To save them wandering hauling laden carts.
Upon these roadways of stumbling let them turn to You,
And dwell within God's Christian pew.

*Denise Shaw*

## THE EYES OF CHRIST

The eyes that wept
As Lazarus slept
The sleep of death in Galilee
Were Jesus' eyes,
The eyes of love,
The eyes of God
From heaven above
Made flesh that He might die for me
O why those eyes
Did men despise
'Til they closed in death on Calvery?
Men still neglect
Those pleading eyes;
They still reject
The sacrifice
Of Christ who died to set them free!

The eyes that cried
When Lazarus died
Run to and fro, o'er earth they gaze;
They probe the hearts
That once despised
The blood, and spurned
The sacrifice
But when He comes those eyes will blaze;
He'll come in might
On charger white,
A blood-soaked vesture His attire;
No time to plead
For mercy then;
Too late indeed
That moment when
His eyes are like a flame of fire!

*Allen S Roberts*

## WOULD WE RECOGNISE HIM

What would they say,
about Jesus now,
if He walked on the earth,
down here below?

Would they mock and scorn,
each and every day,
or would they see,
He's the truth - the way?

Would we follow Him,
if He came here now?
Would we recognise,
the Saviour's love?

We're lucky He came,
here long ago,
and gave His life,
because He loves us so.

*Anna King*

## AND GOD SAW THAT IT WAS GOOD . . .

I wonder what time of day God likes best . . .
If indeed, He is aware of time at all -
Super-physical as He is said to be, transcending the wall
Of the space time continuum.
That said, however, a Lord of all creation
Must know what He has made, the inspiration and expiration
Of a six day labour, according to Genesis.
I have no doubt at all He sees and cares,
And if He is half the God I think He is, I know He shares
All that we feel most keenly, pain, grief, and sorrow -
As we await His known and our much feared tomorrow.
Some of us greet the dawn with joy, others laud the night;
All of us made in His own image - dark and light
Each of us, therefore; as is He, the embodiment of all,
And everything.

Some of us praise at dawn for a new day given;
Others praise at night, seeing the lights of heaven
As souls of angels. Whichever time we choose
To praise Him is His time; only those who refuse
What He has offered, only those who cannot see
Some form of goodness and beauty are not free
To enjoy time.
May peace be theirs,
Somewhere,
Beyond their blindness.

*Jenny Proom*

# THE NUN

She walks with reverence and grace
and heaven shines within her face
she kneels to God in silent prayer
and works the land his crop to bear
the ring she wears upon her hand
is a holy wedding band
up at the pregnant crack of dawn
and then to bed at the close of eve
with a love that never will deceive

*David A Bray*

## FLIGHT OF THE SOUL

Spirit of life do not leave me
   When all that has been is no more.
May I awake to the power of your presence
   Move with you to heaven's gracious shore.
Can the journey be smooth, without effort,
   Will glories unfold on the way,
Colour beyond colour and timeless calm,
   May I speak; or have nothing to say?
Is there silence as a falling rose petal
   Or sweet music I long to embrace,
Can I know a delight only dreamt of
   With the whole of creation in space?
Spirit of life when you lead me
   You and I at last become one,
Lead safely home to my Father God
   And to my Saviour, Jesus, His Son.

***Betty Furneaux***

# DID TIME STAND STILL?

It was half past eight, the wind dropped, I held my breath for a while,
The trees stopped swaying, the howling ceased and I gave a smile.
The clocks have gone back, yet I'm wide awake, a new day is born,
It's windy again, did time stand still between dusk and dawn?
I'm walking to church, my coat's nice and warm I'm pleased to say,
The floor is covered with leaves; they're swirling around,
Once part of a blanket of colour so high, to end life on the ground
Sitting quietly at the middle of a pew,
A smiley face looked at me and asked, 'Can I sit next to you?'
I tried to listen to every word being said, was it meant for me?
Am I clinging to the branches of the ultimate family tree?
The colours I display from day to day,
Is only a fraction of what I'm trying to say.
Summer, autumn, winter, most of all in the spring,
New life begins to surface, out from beneath the weeds, to win.
So the cycle continues, until the time is right,
As we in our faith, fight the good fight.
In reality it's too late to turn the clocks back, each second past has gone,
I pray that I can make a difference in life's long song.
To love and be loved is all that counts on the path that we tread,
Choosing right from wrong, hoping our attitude stands us in good stead.
Drops of rain trickle down the window, forming pools on the ledge,
To be a part of nature's many wonders is their final pledge.
A blade of grass, a feather or a strand of hair,
Each finding its place, to exist, a reason to be there.
Every second, every minute, every hour, every day,
Each star, each cloud, every speck of dust that blows away.
The day we were born the clock began to tick, and became the past,
Then you suddenly realise that your life can't last.
So let's make good use of the time we have, giving thanks for each day.
As we travel on the pathway of God's choosing, we hope and pray.

*Carol Rashid*

## UNTITLED II

Cradle me in your
out stretched arms
letting me know
you're there
Send your Spirit
Fill me now
And touch upon
my heart

Comfort me with
your healing hands
Touch upon my
life
Fill me, with
your love and care
And heal me from the
suffering I bear

Come your Holy
Spirit come
Fill and make
me clean
Drive out all
my dirtiness, Lord
Refresh and make
me new.

***Heather Graham***

## FAITH IN THE LORD

The Lord is my protector
  He is my guiding star
Without the help He gives me
  I could not travel far

He removes life's cruel obstacles
  And nurses me through pain
He knows my weaknesses and my strength
  So with Him I will remain

He taught me all the arts of love
  And how not to let this die
I know He keeps a watch on me
  From His heaven up in the sky

I trust in Him in all I do
  Which keeps my heart at peace
I never will abandon Him
  For I know His love won't cease

*Lachlan Taylor*

# One

When earth holds me in her arms at length,
And death gives me sweet release in sleep,
Do not weep for me.

I shall be one with the dear soil I love
Which, drenched in rain or vital under sun,
Gives me such joy.

Place on my mound the little flowers I love,
Gathered from hedgerows and cool fields,
And let them droop and come to dust upon me.

Bring to me bluebells and pink wild roses,
White ladies bedstraws - and the yellow ones,

That with their mingled scents, and honeysuckles,
They, I and earth may all be one.

*Hilda M Evans*

## MY WORLD AT 1998

I wrote a poem about how my world was, when I was three years old,
But now that I'm ninety a very different tale has to be told.
Today we lock our doors, from the morning till the night,
From dubious strangers, we try to keep out of sight.

For today it matters not, whether you are young or you are old
People on drugs can be cruel and frighteningly bold.
They care not what they do to you, for the blood in their veins runs
                                                                                  cold,
What scares us is that these jailbirds are allowed to be out on parole.

Gone are the teachings we listened to in church,
Good deeds and good manners we kept on a high perch
Today we must not slap the children or use the threatening birch
But sadly, right and wrong are not practised on the hearth.

Science is miraculous if used in the right hands,
But we now have maniacs who make bombs with their dirty hands.
They even blow up babies, who to a long life had a right,
If these madmen watch the aftermath, how can they sleep at night?

Prison sentences to me, are not punishment enough
Criminals should be made to work and live a life that's tough.
And if on their victims they inflicted physical pain
The birch should be used on them, maybe that would make them sane
I'm sure the fear of more lashes would deter them from doing it again.

*Sadie I Williams*

## SKY SCAPES

Painted sky of early morning
With colours softly drawn,
Rose and lilac, duck-egg blue
Artist's palette of the dawn.

The one Celestial Architect
Builds cloud formations fair
The turrets and the battlements
Of castles in the air.

Diamond constellations and
One ruby sparkle bright,
Strewn across black velvet of
The jewel case of the night.

Drama in the thunder and
Storm clouds towering high
Ripped with molten lighting
On the stage-set of the sky.

*Sue Garnett*

## CORCOMROE ABBEY, CO CLARE

At dusk the whisper of sandalled feet, the swish of a monk's attire
who tended the holy fire.
Within ancient abbey walls now other footfalls are heard of modern
pilgrims who no longer bow the knee or remove the shoe,
but wander round and look about and then wend on their way.
We came to Corcomroe on a bright May day, the birds sang and the
valley rang with cuckoo sound, and we were on holy ground,
where centuries ago the flow of prayer and praise was the measure of
their days from dawn to dusk and on again to dawn.
Now that has all gone and only the empty shell remains
where at dusk you can by chance hear upon the air
the whisper of sandalled feet, the swish of a monk's attire
who tended the holy fire.

*B J Smith*

## The Giardino Segreto

I came to you in your sleep
I thought I heard you weeping,
dreams were not enough to keep
me from your side, whilst you were sleeping.

I led you by the hand
through the shuttered window.
The meandering path led through the trees
into the Giardino Segreto.

Terracotta warmed memories
merged with our sorrows indistinct,
the charades we'd played by moonlight
held in the yew hedge, deep and secret.

Around your shoulders hangs the cloak
with jasmine jewels studded white.
Solitary listener to our deepest thoughts,
the heavy manteau of the night.

I will hang around your lovely face
the scented pearls of clematis,
watch you shiver under the moonlight
flicker like a flame in the silver darkness.

The dark green cypress trees
sway us through the woodland glade,
shoulder to shoulder, down to the magic water
where the nightflies masquerade.

I came to you in your sleep
I thought I heard you weeping,
death was not enough to keep
me from your side whilst you were sleeping.

*Nicola Scott*

## THE WINDOW AND THE WALL

That gaunt grey hand that reaches from the grave
More apt to caress then vaporise than to grasp and grin
Take your sword in which there is a word
A word that cuts that false arm down and gives you cause to endure the
turmoil of this life.
For side by side there is the joy and serenity that drowns the strife.
The knowledge that he is your man and that you are his wife.
Finger your fetish - 'tis hard and made of stone,
It grants you your most earnest wish to never be alone.
You were erstwhile in pensive mood on passing thru" your door
So pleased to be back where you stood in your own place once more.
Then as the familiarity waned and you rested in your favourite chair
        The things of life loomed large again -
        and woke your dreads once more.
        Where can we find an all embracing peace
        That can contain our all?
        Have we to through the window gaze -
        or must we face the wall?
When gazing through the window to view the things that live and grow
- the mobile and the fixed in place - indeed, all that you know
Is resolve and truth invested there
Or behind you in the cupboard by the wall?
At times like these you're apt to dwell uncomfortably long - on heaven
and hell.
The ordure of aeons are outside - but are they too within?
Is the soul of this existence made of rust or tin.
That peace that you most earnestly require is neither here or there
Not in the soil or in the treasures hidden in the press that stands against
the wall.

Your God is with you, in spite of all you know.
He will tell you of time - when to come and when to go.
He is not you or even your immortal soul.
He cannot be defined in absolutes if abstracts are the goal.
So be at peace and self contained, your dreams alone are true.
They reside in all that is, not through the window but beyond the wall.

**Ray Foot**

## ALONE

Walk not away,
    at such a time.
My pain and sorrow,
    too hard to bear.
Alone.
Put your hand in mine,
and hold me more gently,
    show me you care.

Turn not your face,
    at such a time.
Look on my grief,
    too hard to bear.
Alone.
Bring me some comfort,
and speak to me softly,
    show me you care.

I once gave love,
    at such a time.
Now mine the need,
    too hard to bear.
Alone.
Give me that love,
and handle me tenderly,
    show me you care.

My soul now lies open,
    at such a time.
My need to intense,
    too hard to bear.
Alone.
Pray for my kindly,
and judge me not harshly,
    show me you care.

**A Pollock**

# The Lamb

Lamb of eternity, chosen by Father,
Delight of Godhead, Word all-creating,
In his own Life-Book sovereignly writing
Names of foreknown, predestined, called, justified.

Lamb sent to stable straw, convoyed by angels,
Wonderful God-Man, Word flesh-becoming,
By divine world-love humanly sharing,
Came to his own, rejected, snubbed, vilified.

Lamb on the rugged cross, wounded by sinners,
Sacrifice God-sent, Word whole-fulfilling,
Through potent life-blood completely saving,
Suffered alone, disfigured, stripped, crucified.

Lamb - focus of cosmos, worshipped by myriads,
Son God-exalted, Word sin-defeating,
With his prized Church-Bride timelessly reigning
On heaven's throne, rewarded, changed, glorified.

*Leslie Emmett*

## FAITH TO SEE

I have a friend who does not see
And yet in darkness cannot be,
For he has lost more than his sight
Yet walks with Jesus as his light.

Yes every night and every day
Hand in hand along the way,
Thanking Jesus for his grace
And helping others to this place.

But is he bitter, sad or down?
And does he wear a daily frown?
No my friend lives in hope
That Jesus gives him strength to cope.

At times he sees much more than I
Sometimes he knows when others cry,
Where does he get the strength to live
And most of all the love to give.

'It's Jesus', who gives me sight
In darkest day or darkest night,
To him who died that I might live
My spirit, soul and body give.

On this we both see eye to eye
And often talk of times gone by,
For sure we know one day he'll see
Until that time content he'll be.

Content that Jesus Christ is *King*
And of his praises *Daily Sing,*
So Satan raise your head and hiss
You won't defeat my friend, Chris.

*Terry Russell*

## THE WONDER OF THE RAINBOW

When you see a rainbow stretched out across the sky -
Do you ever wonder when or how or why?
This lovely band of coloured hues was placed up there for us,
Well if you will just listen; I will tell how God above -came to create
this wonder all because of His great love,
I'm sure you've heard of Noah. He's the man who built the ark,
He lived when violence was everywhere, and things were very dark -
Now Noah and his family were all the people God could find,
who listened when He told them what He had in mind;
He said that because of all the darkness, He would have to send a flood
and it broke God's heart to do it, but Noah understood.
After it was over Noah's family emerged, to find that all the earth
had been give a New Birth.
Then God created for us a rainbow, to remind Him of His love;
and His promise made to Noah, when he sees this wonder up above
that never again will He destroy the earth with a devastating flood.
*So* next time you see a rainbow stretched across the sky,
I hope it will remind you of The Mighty God above who did create
The rainbow to show to us His love . . .

*Margaret Wood*

## My Dream

My vision is one day I'll see
The children of this land
Walk side by side down every street
Joined each one hand in hand.

Walking steadfast ever forward
To each their chosen goal
Singing 'On To Jesus Onward'
Each one a joyful soul.

Their eyes will light up pathways
Their singing ring like bells
And all their laughter echo
O'er streets and hills and fells.

I want to hear them chatter
'Bout Jesus and His love
Of all the things He wants for them
About the home He's made above.

I love to hear them chanting,
'Hallelujah! Praise the Lord'
To hear them shouting 'Onward.'
Their minds of one accord.

No more will they go hungry,
Not one will thirst again.
They'll drink the living waters
And feast on father's grain.

They'll never feel the cold again,
Or want for earthly things,
All needs will be forgotten
Their cares will all have wings.

No child will be neglected,
Or left to seek His place.
Our Jesus loves His children
They see love in His face.

*Alma Taylor*

# A Tribute To Life

On bended knee I say a prayer of thanks to Him above,
For all the wondrous beauty, that expresses His great love
Remember His Redeemer Son, His lifetime torn by strife
Let's thank Him very humbly, for the precious gift of life.

Give thanks for natures wonders, the beauty of the trees
The joy of hearing birds that sing, the humming of the bees
The fish that swim around the seas, all wonders to behold
Or desert sands and changing climes, that's shaped the earthly mould.

Give praise to all the joyful things that give us daily pleasure
The days when sunshine brings to life, enchantment to our leisure
The wildlife on the hillside walks, or plant-life by the river
These treats of nature clearly show, how generous is our giver.

On winter nights when evenings bright are lit by moon and stars
Orion, Bear and Cygnet Swan, or planets Venus, Mars
All have their place along with Earth, all with their orbits sealed
And held in place in outer space, in worlds magnetic field.

As we look ever forward, to the beauties of the Spring
The colour of the flowers and shrubs that changing seasons bring
As children of the Universe, we watch the years unfold
And wonder, at the greatest living story ever told.

*Charles N Smith*

## Meeting

Walking down Oxford Street, in a daze of my own
Weaving in and out, as thread upon a loom.
A vast variety of unknown faces,
Blend into one.
A string of knots inside my head,
A reminder - of unaccomplished matters,
Pressing harder - on my already overcrowded mind.
Somewhere out of this chaos and confusion
Both inside and out, a picture is emerging.
There is a shout - I hear my name!
Yes it's repeated again
Who is it? That recognises me among so many?
Calling me forth.
Eager to know I swiftly scan a limited horizon.
Standing three paces distance,
I see familiarity!
A smile of recognition.
Father, it's good to see you.
Reaching out connecting with an embrace;
Of all that has flowed in-between the previous encounter (It says it all)
> 'Father I have sinned against heaven and against you
> I no longer deserve to be called your Son.'

Still I am, through your constant, unfailing love,
Which I've met; yet again today.

*Margaret Oldman*

## I Come To The Cross

When I am lonely and weak in faith,
burdened with troubles,
I bow my head in shame.
When my actions have been misunderstood,
and I wonder from your glory.
I take a breath,
and close my eyes to pray
Sometimes only for a few minutes in a day,
but those minutes are mine,
and I cherish them with all of my heart.
For it is then that your Spirit comes to me,
and I receive your precious peace and joy.
I ask for your forgiveness,
and humble myself.
Here I stand before you Lord,
A weak and feeble body.
Then I see the rugged cross.
The emblem of suffering and shame.
Here my chains are broken.
My burdens left to rest,
and I can stand once more,
To proclaim your Holy Name.

*Nicky Freeman*

## HAVE YOU EVER BEEN CRUCIFIED

'Have you?'
Do you know what it's like to hang there on a cross.
Exposed for all the world to see; taking centre stage
and having the spotlight full on you.
'Well do you?'

Do you know what it's like when your close friends desert you.
Is your name Peter also, are you waiting for the cock to crow.
'Well are you?'

'Or are you Pilate, with nice clean hands?'

Do you know what it's like to be naked to the world.
'Well do you?'

Have you ever felt the pain of thorns upon your head, or
heard the insults and abuse from the crowds.
'Well have you?'

Have you carried your cross through the hostile streets
and fallen under its weight, or stumbled and felt no helping hands.
'Have you?'

Please don't say; I know the way 'you feel'.

Have you stretched out your hands ready for the nails.
'Well *have you*?'
Have you felt the isolation of hanging on a cross.
And thought it was a gain and not a loss.
'Have you?'

Have you hung there in full view for all the world to see.
Have you been Crucified like *Jesus*, who did it all for me.
'Well have you?'

***Pax***

## CHRISTMAS THOUGHTS

Christmastime is a time of fun
Scurrying around. Look at everyone
Shopping for Ann and Bob and Kate
Auntie and Granda and Gran. It's great.

What's for dinner? Turkey and sprouts!
'We want some trifle,' the children shout.
A nice pair of slippers for Mum, she's worked hard
A shirt and tie and some hankies for Dad.

Christmas morning. Has Santa arrived?
'Let's all go and see. Oh! What a surprise,
That's just what I asked for, and look, there's lots more
Scattered about on the chairs and the floor.'

But let's stop for a moment, let's think for a while
Two thousand years ago, there was born a boy child
No room at the Inn. In a manger he lay
No fancy duvet, but a stall full of hay.

Yes, sure there were presents, rich spices and gold
Each were laid on the floor, for so it was told.
But the greatest of gifts was Jesus, The Lamb,
God sent Him from Heaven, the Son of Man.

He came to bring peace and goodwill to all men
Let's remember the reason we celebrate then
Christmas is Christ's birthday, so let's bow down and pray
'Thank you Lord for this gift of Your Son in that way.'

Yes it's nice to give gifts to the people we love
But don't ever forget about God up above
Remember His precious gift on that first Christmas morn'
Was announced by an angel. 'Christ the Saviour is born.'

**Gordon Roberts**

### THE YOUNG RULER

Thoughts of eternity lead me to Him
On hands and knees,
my body burdened with luggage.

Let me take it

The closer I get the heavier it becomes
I refuse to let it go.
Fear of the uncertain stops me
Crushed beneath the weight of an infinite nothingness I face life trapped
here
midway between the almighty and darkness
in the void between Heaven and Hell
called Earth

*Scott Moray Williamson*

## HE CALLED HIM DAD

Joseph was a man specially chosen
Husband of Mary, father to Jesus
He grew up admiring him
Strong, gentle, wise.
Still a child, He watched him work, fascinated
His wood-roughened hands gently lifted Him
And placed Him in vantage position
Older, He learned his craft.
They shared their hopes, their dreams,
He called him Dad.

*Gerry McColl*

## ISLAND OF DREAMS

Do you remember our long ago dream
Of a world of our own, set out at sea,
Amongst foaming blue waves and coral reefs
In a place untarnished, our island would be.

Below a blue sky with sun smiling down
Caressing the sand with its tender beams,
Would be you and I, like Adam and Eve,
In God's greatest creation, the island of dreams.

We wanted our very own Niagara,
And beautiful flowers like Babylon,
And all the stars shining bright above us;
God's greatest creations, all rolled in one.

Majestic mountains, and deep dark caves,
Dreams of nature uncaged and free,
Rivers running unpolluted to the sea,
No violence, or bloodshed, just harmony.

What happened to that long ago dream?
Grey buildings now stretch as far as we see,
Our island replaced by a concrete jungle.
God's greatest creation? You tell me.

*Katie Shilton*

## ΦΩΣΙΛΑΡΟΝ
*(A Hymn for Compline)*

With the fading of sun's rays
The passing of the light
The coming of the kindly rest of night
Reminder of the shortness of man's days
We thank you for the One you sent
To pierce the darkness, heal the discontent
Of our day's noon.

Soon may your light return
Raise us, forgiven, new
With hearts that burn to praise
You who alone can bring
Light and life everlasting.

**Jack B Lynn**

## Galashiels

In Galashiels, it almost feels,
Like winter's in the air.
The summer fades and autumn shades,
Just make you want to stare.
The brown and yellow, red and gold,
The feel of time, a scene so old.
The generations come and go,
And silent shrouded in the snow,
I stand amazed that we could know
Such peace within this world.

And as the icy raindrops fall,
Beneath the tree we stand
We gaze out through the mist and rain
Across the windswept land
The rain is falling softer now
To walk away I don't know how.
We meditate on what we see
And dream of what someday there'll be
And what we'll share eternally
Such peace within this world.

*Darryl Williams*

## WHEN THE SPARROW FALLS

*This was first written in memory of my brother's first hero, the footballer, Davie Cooper who died on 23/3/95 and for many ordinary folk who have passed away without knowing a higher way for whom God weeps . . .*
*For whether we are heroes or the boy next door, we are all loved. That's why Christ died.*
*'Aren't five sparrows sold for two pennies? Yet not one sparrow is forgotten by God' Matthew: Chapter 10, Verse 29*

A single sparrow's fallen,
but does anybody care?
It was special, now it's fallen,
and we pass by unaware.

Or we stop, just for a moment,
shake our heads and then move on.
We *are* sorry that it's fallen,
But it's too late now it's gone.

But God weeps for that one sparrow,
As He grieves for each life lost,
For He made a way to save them,
And He paid the highest cost.

And for each life now that's purchased
by the blood of God's own Son,
He expects us all to care, and share
His love with *everyone!*

We must learn to love each sparrow,
Try to show it where to fly.
For it may just be a sparrow
But it's special in God's eyes.

*Alison Murphy*

## LIFE

A new beginning -
Baby in the womb;
Child of God; - listening to
The heartbeat of your
Mother, father, - both in one.
Complete in faith;
Complete in trust;
So clear is conception,
Pouring life into growth
All at its own pace,
Undisturbed by the outside world.

A silent world of communication,
Simplicity itself, but as yet, incomplete.

Love is feeding
At the breast of mankind.
Sometimes sorrow, sometimes joy, appears.
In the midst of
Confusion, anger, frustration,
Peace arrives;
And love starts to flow
From within;
Feeding on the eternal Word,
Jesus, hidden in the flesh
Of our humanity.

He is revealed as the way
Expressed in the freedom to love.

*Sheila Cundy*

## THE LIVING CHURCH

People think of churches as being made
of brick and stone
What they fail to realise is they're not
built of that alone,
A church consists of people working hand
in hand
Who toil to lead a Christian life and live
by God's command,
Each one is like a building brick that faith
binds fast together
True fellowship becomes the roof that braves
all kinds of weather
And eyes and hearts raised up to God become
the tower and steeple
The church that stands the test of time is
made of God's own people.

*Margaret McTavish*

## HERE ON THE GROUND

With Heaven above
Here, on the ground,
Each aspect of all beauty's found,
From single leaf to full-grown trees,
Snowflakes drifting in winter's breeze.
Whether you look afar or near
Nature's splendedness is clear.
In landscape, brook or butterfly wing
Beauty's there - in everything,
So give great thanks to be alive
And pray all nature does survive.

God made the world in such a way
All living things enjoy it,
Let's take great care, we all must say,
That man does not destroy it.

*George A Tanner*

## LAZY

Neighbours nosing over the fence say I'm lazy.
My garden is simple, untouched.
Who am I to tame its rugged
beauty, as the grass grows like a pubescent teenager - swiftly upwards
reaching for the future.
Gardens march away on either side in row upon row of uniform
prettiness.
Not for them are weeds roaming
unhindered as wild stallions.
There, nature as performing lion is tamed for the enjoyment
of the spectator.
The lavender is contained by the bridle of human restraint,
the daisies scared to sleep in case of eviction, the privet
plucked and preened into a regimented shape - like the pansy lanes
cries out for freedom.
Me, I let my garden have its liberty,
I'm not lazy . . .
I'm just leaving it to the Lord.

*Kirsty Duncombe*

## THE GARDEN SONG

My heart is at peace whenever I sit
In a garden all alone
Surrounded by flowers, by shrubs and by trees
It melts my hard heart of stone.
My peace is so perfect I must declare
Lord, thanks for a garden so lovely and fair.

The dark coloured leaves remind me of sin
Of the things that I've done wrong,
The anger, the hurt and the pain I've caused
It's the sad part of this song
So Heavenly Father please hear my prayer
Lord, thanks for a garden so lovely and fair.

The next thing I see, the wood of the tree
The trunk so upright and tall
It tells me of Jesus, hung there on the Cross
His life sacrificed for all.
So then in thanksgiving I must declare
Lord, thanks for a garden so lovely and fair.

The red of the rose shouts clearly to me
Of the blood of Jesus spilled
Forgiveness is mine, and when I repent
Then life can be Spirit filled.
And so in repentance I bring this prayer
Lord, thanks for a garden so lovely and fair.

But the overall picture that I see
While I'm in that garden fair
Is a beautiful scene of God in Heaven
Most anxious to meet me there.
So then in rejoicing I must declare
Lord, thanks for a garden so lovely and fair.

*Gordon Baillie*

## WHERE WILD BIRDS CRY

For weeks, in pouring rain
Or burning sun, he'd laboured,
Digging out, by hand,
His monitoring chambers
Which will, in time, he filled with water
Spoilt by man.

Side by side they lie
Encased in wood,
Bottomed out with pea-gravel
And set with reeds.
Modern technology will show his readings
Unknown to ancient man
But ancient man had not polluted
The element - water
As modern man has done
We need his foresight, dedication
A quiet, unassuring youngster;
My own hope for the planet's future and mankind
The epitome, for me, of dreams
As yet unrealised.
A spirit soaring free
Above the evils of this world
A non-destructed.

Ageless, timeless, the thread of love and perseverance
Clings precariously to spade, and gadget
Reading signs and potent
hidden to the naked eye
On an exposed Welsh working wild birds calling
The wind crying down the centuries of learning
He works alone.

*Helen Perry*

### AIRBORNE

Never lingering, never anticipating,
with outstretched wings
to catch the wind
the earthborns cannot see
yet are left wondering from whence
the source of flight.
Without dullness or anxiety,
each moment created in an instant
where past and future meet
and passivity echoes a much richer note
to leave the hearers rapt
with the beauty of its peace.

*Irvin S-Allen*

## MYSTERIES OF LIFE

When life is full of sunshine
Then calm waters ever flow,
Smooth be the roads to walk on
Such radiance, warmth must glow.

Alas these storms and tempests
Come raging troubles to bring.
So rough the path, great hardship
Such secrets of life learning.

Through pain and tribulation
Inner strength of each new day,
Immense courage to endure
With hope in your heart alway.

Hold on to faith eternal
Sweet victory soon to reach
Believe, triumph in glory
Lord, such wisdom we beseech.

Then stronger for our journeys
Your spirit to shine so bright.
We pray for understanding
Our Saviour, infinite light.

The past is gone go forward
Mysteries of life to share
Wonderful gifts surround you
Feel God's love just everywhere.

*Margaret Jackson*

## GOD PROMISES PEACE ON EARTH

I've heard that the world is passing away,
Does that mean mankind no longer on earth will stay?
Indeed not! Jesus' ransom sacrifice,
Gave humans the chance of everlasting life.

God will bring to an end the world of wickedness and sin
No longer will wars be fought and living be grim
The earth remains forever with no pollution or fear
All will live peacefully together, year after year.

We'll be ruled by Jesus Christ as King,
For a thousand years to perfection bring
Each man, woman, child and babe, never again
Experiencing sickness, sorrow, death or pain.

Our voices are raised in joy and thanksgiving
To praise our God Jehovah for our chance of living
We'll be surrounded by God's cleansed earth
And each day be full of satisfaction and mirth.

*Ellen Cooke*

## CANDLEMASS
## THE FEAST OF THE
## PURIFICATION OF THE VIRGIN

Today, along a neighbouring street,
Beneath the rotten leaves and frosted weeds
Which lengthy winter has not yet destroyed,
I saw the first snowdrops.

Fragile, vulnerable,
Like milk-filled breasts they hung,
Caressed by their own foliage.
It seemed as if the whole earth
were struggling to give birth.

'Mary's Candles' they call them here.
A fragile flicker in the dark;
Angelic heralds
Of the Light to come.

***Christine Mylne***

# INFORMATION

We hope you have enjoyed reading this book - and that you will continue to enjoy it in the coming years.

If you like reading and writing poetry drop us a line, or give us a call, and we'll send you a free information pack.

Write to :-
**Triumph House Information
1-2 Wainman Road
Woodston
Peterborough
PE2 7BU
(01733) 230749**